IN BETWEEN FAITH

IN BETWEEN FAITH

Dana L. Stringer

Black Picket Fence
A Publishing Company

Black Picket Fence
P.O. Box 1532
Roswell, GA 30077-1532

Copyright © 2014 by Dana L. Stringer
All rights reserved.
Printed in the United States of America

First Edition, 2014

ISBN 978-0-9915349-0-6 (paperbound)

Library of Congress Cataloging in Publication Data:
Stringer, Dana
In Between Faith / Dana Stringer
Library of Congress Control Number: 2014933185

Dedicated to those who remain in between faith.

And straightway the father of the child cried out, and said with tears, Lord, I believe; help thou mine unbelief.

                        Mark 9:24, King James Bible

Table of Contents

in between faith 1
after the cock crows 2
amen 3
balm 4
casting stones 5
club zin 6
confession 8
cover up 9
drought 10
ego 11
epistle 12
eve's drop 13
evensong to my ancestors 14
flash 15
foe 16
for God and country 17
holy dance 18
human 19
laden 20
master's gospel 21
mister sinner man 22
old-time religion 23
parable 24

pass the cup	25
prodigal	26
radical	27
revival	28
sparrow	29
suicide's watch	30
temptress	31
testament	32
visit to a virgin	33
vow	34
1-800-blessing	35
what if	36
whooping and hollering	37
witness	38
wretch like me	39
coming home	40
rebirth	41

Acknowledgements

I am most grateful to God who granted me the liberty to explore my questions, my concerns, and my doubts through the craft of writing.

I am deeply grateful for my parents who continue to love and support me through every season and every transition in my life.

Special thanks to Douglas Kearney who helped me to get the majority of these poems to where they needed to be.

in between faith

I am one of many
sliding back
through the navel
and into the belly of hell
wedged between a psalm
and a dirty joke
I am cain killing abel
jacob deceiving esau
judas betraying jesus
I am twin heads talking
two tales told
I am both beams
of the cross

after the cock crows

he rises to face his flock
marks where their stones have landed

the pulpit shrinks beneath his feet
as the sun sets inside his gut

he feels the bondage of breathing
when outrage members render him guilty

he befriended a queer pastor
and permitted him to speak at his church

in an open letter to his followers
he denies knowing the man was that way

he atones himself with an apology
and saves himself from judgment

amen

I watch unwed women
half a century old
their wide thighs plastered
to padded pews
heavy hands and church fans
wave away hot flashes
in between *praise the lord*
and *amen*

their legs are crossed
tighter than their fingers
like twisted wishbones
eager to break
for matrimony

a man of the cloth
covers their homes
fills the unclaimed shoes
of absentee men
crosses thresholds into prison
wards to sermonize boys caged
inside the bodies of men

he prophesies husbands
eulogizes sons
while women tarry
cleaving to their bibles
before the laying on of hands
for a blessing

balm

I have fought
one thousand fights
died almost twice
even prayed to once
cease to be
and then come back
topple my headstone
betray death and the grave
in search for a balm
not to heal afflictions
from sticks or stones
that didn't hurt
but for religion
this infirmity in my bones

casting stones

these are your sons
lost boys of the altar
their feet laced
in shiny church shoes
camouflaging their paths
away from good wives

these wayward sheep
creep beneath city lights
and pink neon blinking above
leather-clad mannequins
leashed behind plated glass

rodded men lead them
down alleys littered
with used condoms
and dry seed to satisfy
needs that go unmet
in prayer

but who will judge
this down low gospel
when they return
to their pulpits
to throw more stones

club zin

cigarette smoke worms above
a patio of strangers
paying homage to the gods
of heat lamps and hennessey

I pan a crowd
of unfamiliar faces
their fake smiles break
into shallow laughter

he is sitting as she
cross-dressed cross-legged
sipping white zin
muting his *glory hallelujahs*

I cradle and nurse
my cocktail while his eyes peruse
the place for cocks and tails
ready to serve and be served

his thin dark frame
forces stares
from prowling cats waiting
for their cue to pounce

our eyes meet
we pretend they don't
and play strangers in a place
where our truth is set free

come sunday he marches
in with the choir
back arched chin high
speaking in tongues
clutching his bible
like a brand new handbag

confession

father forgive me for I am taking her
the way I want to be taken by him
but I am not supposed to say that
I am a married man
haunted by family portrait eyes
staring out from a frame
propped upon the nightstand
the clock ticks between her moans
the headboard pounds
against the wall and I imagine
his breath blowing down my spine
my body splayed like a wild animal rug
while I obey his commands for more of me
father forgive me for coveting that
piece of him inside of me
for better and for worse

cover up

secrets go bump
behind these walls
eyes see what lips can't utter
for man's sake and his name
every mouth stays shut
except for an old church mouse
squeaking inside a closet
full of bones
rotting underneath
a pile of dirty cassocks

drought

I can take you to a place
where dry tongues wag
between cracked lips
underneath murals of moses
parting the red sea
noah drifting the deep
and john dipping gentiles
in the river jordan
while jesus crosses over
a drained baptismal pool

ego

watch him
voracious
fed by a crescendo of praises
ascending the pews
the pulpit
his howl goes unchecked

listen to the lambs all a-cryin'
listen to the lambs all a-cryin'

hands clap tambourines clang
before the beast
fleeces his flock
a glutton for more than lamb chops
all bow at the altar
as he preys

listen to the lambs all a-cryin'
listen to the lambs all a-cryin'

undercover him and see
what big eyes he got
what big name he got
what big church he built
what big car he drives

listen to the lambs all a-cryin'
listen to the lambs all a-cryin'

epistle

dear saints

I am not that glittered face glowing on the mardi gras float in the pride parade or the well-oiled, topless body tattooed with cobras and mermaids

I am not that tomboy in the black fedora and a pinstriped vest concealing taped down breasts

I am not that defiant dyke camped at the bottom of courthouse steps cursing under a cardboard sign written in all caps

I am not that man waiting inside a black sedan with an opened zipper and an unlocked door

I am not that tight-assed twink pirouetting in a pink tutu in a dance studio downtown

I am not that brown-toothed pedophile with children's toys, hard candy, and rope stuffed inside a dirty red duffle bag in the back seat

I am a believer wearing a crooked mask
of a straight saint sitting on the third pew

eve's drop

here we are at the tree
its bent branches
a shredded umbrella
for our blanched bodies
but I have not known adam
his brawny back incessantly turned
helel comes
and coils himself around me
spiraling down like a scaly vine
to feed upon the fruit
in my untilled garden
reaping it with his forked tongue
if only adam would turn to see
this feast of figs and love

evensong to my ancestors

I pray you send me the ghost
that holy one
you kept shut inside your bones
who gave us spirituals and tongues
and unbreakable spirits
under the mighty lash of a whip
that could part the mississippi
until kingdom come
and kumbayah was remixed
may that holy one
bestow upon me the gift
of uncircumcised otherness
with an ear to hear
your voices speaking from the grave
may that ghost
set my tongue on fire
make my words the antagonist
of assimilation
while I await the second coming

flash

vanity's mirror reflects
a dark-skinned physique

posing inside the lens
a muscle-bound bishop

bulges in spandex
for fatherless boys

but money goes where
the mouth has been

so an animal can return
safely into the wild

foe

I met the devil in church
no sharp fangs stained yellow
no horns protruding from his skull
no sixes tattooed on his forehead
no red serpentine tail
wrapped around a pitchfork
no bits of flesh decaying
underneath black fingernails
or beady bloodshot eyes peering out
from behind a curtain of flames
I met the devil in church
he was dressed in a tailor-made suit
polished and sparkling like a star

for God and country

if I get too close I can see
the confederate flag
at full staff
flapping inside his pupils
a cross on fire
in a southern field
hounds sniffing out a nigger
torch lights and shotguns
a noose
a tree
black body
white mob
onward christian soldier

holy dance

I am the angel
that fell
between the crack
of two piano keys
and waited for the choir
to stop singing
but a big lady
and her blue past
began to dance
in a small circle
of divine shouts
holding her hipbone
when her feet caught fire
and moved her
down the aisle
across the altar
past the preacher
sweating out God
shouts
kept rising over
half-cocked church hats
rocking in sync
with babies cradled
in the arms
of mothers
while I clung
to the minor key

human

remember that heap of dirt
piled inside God's unlined palm
the unseen mouth opening
and blowing us into beings

remember our bodies of clay
growing limbs, frolicking
in a field of unnamed things
shortly after the beginning

remember we grew tired
and slept in between the angels
and dreamed of being human
after we failed as gods

laden

they were more heavy than deep
cradling burdens close to their bosoms
like overgrown babies unburped
these weary mothers
of wayward children
crowded at the altar
of the half-lit sanctuary
wrestling their miracles
from the hand of God

master's gospel

say we were pagans
hell bound heathens drowning
in a flood of feces and piss
down in the dark bowels
of a dutch ship

say we were descendants
of ham—bad seeds
to be sold and sowed
in cotton fields
way over yonder

say we were wild-eyed
savages, sealed with a fate
of field hand
free laborers
to work stolen land

say we dipped our bodies
into brushwood, crossed dirt
roads, followed oil lanterns
down twig-filled trails
into the hush harbor

say we came this far by faith
but mostly by fear
of a master who bound us
to this gospel

mister sinner man

I saw you near the crossroads
cursing spirits in the bottom
of a bottle wrapped
inside a brown paper bag
you were bent
beneath the moon's light
christening the ground
beside a naked tree
I watched you
walk on yellow water
in unlaced shoes
that only christ would tie

old-time religion

moist palms move down her backside slow
she smoothes her house dress
before sitting down
on the wooden bench at her organ
her wrinkled fingers
flip several pages of the songbook
blessed assurance
the old rugged cross
the tips of her aged fingers rest
upon the keys
notes seep through the pores
of the front screened door
a neighbor sways to salvation's song
I sit near the edge of her red velvet sofa
staring at an oversized bible on the table
jesus gazes out from its cover
a circle of soft yellow light crowns his head
I reach out for grandmother's old-time religion
wondering if it's good enough for me

parable

I am carrying a white bucket
and wading through a river
of black fish
speckled with bright yellow spots
I catch them one by one
with my right hand
while they try to flop free
from my grip
their little black faces are marked
with fear of being caught
inside the white trap

pass the cup

I was just a lamb
little but not mary's
all wide-eyed and woolly-haired
with boney arms and skinny legs
flapping in a west end wind
chasing the church bus
bound for bible school
I was more baptist than missionary
all crayons and crosses
bible stories and butter cookies
served with fruit punch
sweet like the kool-aid
every black child loves to drink

prodigal

I am a good sister while I'm here
chewing on a wafer
sipping grape juice
at communion's table
and feasting on the words
of traveling prophets

I am a good sister while I'm here
fighting the good fight
naming it claiming it
rolling holy like a wheel
in the middle of a wheel
across the backside of the desert

I am a bad sister when I stray
from the table
leave the ninety-nine
to go revel in the valley
of black sheep
bucking bad shepherds

radical

citizens are under siege
by a street prophet
armed with a bullhorn
and a bible
launching an attack
with scriptures and rage
upon pedestrians passing
inside the public square
no peace for the wicked
he fires rounds of free speech
a catastrophe with casualties
of biblical proportions

revival

this was not just a happening
no time or date typeset with fancy fonts
inside the church bulletin
no announcement saturated in hyperbole
across gospel stations to lure the amen crowd
before video could capture
and stream sermons in real-time
the Spirit moved like wildfire
and consumed us like uncleared brush
with unrepentant flames
long lines stood outside
waiting to be touched by God
it was a stirring
a troubling of the water
a blaze inside the bones
shaking and jerking
we couldn't stop
we didn't leave
we kept drinking
we kept burning

sparrow

mahalia jackson's contralto voice carried us
like a mother carries a fetus inside her womb but
through back doors to rear sections of jim crow places
past lunch counters wiped clean
of black faces
it bore us up
under the weight of wrong as we watched
maimed flesh dangling from branches
it strengthened us
after every blow from the billy club
as leashed dogs barked us back into second class
it renewed us
after the water hose drenched us unequal
it marched us
to washington to selma to montgomery and back
it kept rosa in her seat
we sing
not because we're happy but because we have to

suicide's watch

the red hand ticks
toward twelve
like a time bomb
barefoot
ice blue body hangs
from the basement ceiling
of an old church
his tongue
like a dead slug
between stiff white lips
a sticky note
stuck to his shirt
gay teen lost
on the road
to straight and narrow

temptress

salome is like jezebel
her tease is tamed
the tarnished crowns of kings
lay at her feet
their brute bodies lie
slain between her legs
their power compromised
inside her bedchamber
from her belly's dance
hips that cast spells
a tongue that bewitches
them into pieces
before serving their heads
on silver platters

testament

this is my story
it is not a song
once upon a time
in the beginning
everything almost was
then it wasn't
and that nearly killed me
so I inked out an existence
from one margin
to the next
knowing I was this
while expected to be that
then praying to become
something
that left me doubting
I could ever be
a happy ending

visit to a virgin

no oversized arm stretched down from heaven
to pull the girl away from the overworked hand
with over bitten nails feeling its way underneath
the blanket to unlock her twelve-year old legs
no nail-scarred hand ripped away the rooftop
to catch the lone tear that fell and dried
in the center of her right cheek
just thick brown fingers with hard knuckles
rubbing over a small patch of her puberty
as she swallowed her voice in the dark
waiting on christ to split the sky
and pry him off her body lying parallel to hell
and although the thrust inside her thighs
wasn't like the spear piercing christ's side
blood still crept down her leg like a red snake

vow

I wonder if God watches
from above
that bishop bowing his head
clasping a crucifix
that nun twisting beads
and hailing mary
that priest washing
and wringing his hands
that altar boy wiping his mouth
vowing not to tell

1-800-blessing

it's always after midnight
when operators are standing by
a fiery preacher
pleading with viewers
to act fast
call the number on the screen
before airtime runs out
when God locks the gates
to the promised land
and closes the windows of heaven
do not miss this opportunity
write a check
payable to: man of God
wait for a small vial
of miracle spring water
a personalized prophesy
and a special prayer cloth
coming in the mail
but no money back
guarantee

what if

Jesus is black
and all men cleanse
their sins in the blood
of a brother
we bow down to worship
at his big dark feet
cleave to the cross
of a colored man
ask for forgiveness
then wait for him
to return like a thief
in the night

whooping and hollering

I can time it all
preacher gasps
between baritone moans
composed inside gut moving
up through throat
exploding out mouth
bald head tilted back
weight balanced on left foot
right one lifted to stomp
sleeves of robe flapping
like bat wings
sounds from hammond b3
shouts echoing from choir stand
monogrammed handkerchief
balled inside sweaty black fist
airborne saliva traveling south
winding down
catching breath
closing bible
altar call
eyes shifting toward sinners
benediction
doors of church opening

witness

the last two drags on the cigarette are slow
my puffy eyes watch thin streams of smoke
circle around streaks of moonlight leaking
through slits in the mini blinds
slicing the unlit room
I inhale a smoky ache deep into my lungs
and cough out an ultimatum to the almighty
kill me or change me but I won't live a double life
I crawl to the window
the carpet crushing under my knees
here's some second-hand hope
from your jilted bible thumper
I release a puff and wait for a bolt of lightning
to divide the sky but the stars just spy like angels
a cricket chirps from the untrimmed bushes below
a matted mutt whimpers up the alley
the ceiling fan drones low
my eyes meander over terracotta rooftops
and down an empty dead end street
my knees buckle and I collapse
with my head facing the opened closet

wretch like me

cold stares pierce me
like an arrowhead
I'm baring skin
a thou shalt not

whispers waltz behind my back
I sashay down the aisle
in open-toe shoes
busy minds of boys misbehave

my thick hips twist
my big lips tempt
godly men weaken with want
halos shake a shame-on-me

fingers point
like clean needles
my dress is too short
neckline too low

my earrings cling
my bracelets clang
disturbing the righteous
how sweet the sound

coming home

chimes of church bells resound
breaking morning's stillness
saintly strangers depart from dwellings
scurrying toward stained-glass hope

a borrowed bible in hand I mount the steps
a white-gloved greeter ushers me forth
I lift my head high before marching in
to find a seat in the house of promises

rebirth

an ache leavens inside my womb
crests
at the crown of my throat
wrestles
my bridled tongue loose

my voice labors for a song
begets
a psalm surrendering my soul
chest
opens and melts the stone

light splits my spirit from
flesh
marrow from bone
rest
in between two worlds known

You may visit:
www.danastringer.com

www.ingramcontent.com/pod-product-compliance
Lightning Source LLC
Chambersburg PA
CBHW032052290426
44110CB00012B/1058